AF505952

SIGN

AHSAHTA PRESS

The New Series

NUMBER 20

SIGN

David Mutschlecner

BOISE STATE UNIVERSITY · BOISE · IDAHO · 2007

Ahsahta Press, Boise State University
Boise, Idaho 83725
http://ahsahtapress.boisestate.edu

First printing September 2007
ISBN-13: 978-0-916272-96-8

Library of Congress Cataloging-in-Publication Data

Mutschlecner, David.
 Sign / David Mutschlecner.
     p. cm. -- (The new series ; no. 20)
 ISBN 978-0-916272-96-8 (pbk. : alk. paper)
 I. Title.

PS3563.U855S57 2007
811'.54--DC22

                    2007011816

The author would like to thank Rob Hipwood and Matt Pierce.

FOR CELIA AND TIM

CONTENTS

PART I

THE NIGHT WATCH

*Speak back
into the spark of me
the line
where three
words meet*

*for a dissonance
subtends the self.*

*

I came at night
to see his face shine.

*

A priest
shook
over a king

red
exhalation,

a mist of blood.

What is now said
in the same breath?

*

God
man
lamb—

what steps out from the stony law.

*

Time lives only when it knows
its end.

Time
fell asleep in the law.

*

Incantation equation—

a nose cone whose blown-back thought balloon
can no longer be read

I,
the night-watch,
speak for you
in your calculated future.

*

I was at the edge of a circle
looking in.

I had again
come to him in the dark.

Blood beyond the line
my feet touched.

*

Pauper thought
takes the throne of wisdom,

lamplight
that shows only
how deep the dark.

*

Night wind. All rigor
becomes roil
in the pitch
cauldron of the firmament.

*

Welter of flesh and blood suspended

broke time's
parabola,

a burning white oath
upon the eyes—
as Moses lifted up
the serpent in the desert.

*

You in your future!

Can you not take grace
into your quick
strictures?

*

Ask the skull a question.

All hold Golgotha in their hands.

IN NEBUCHADNEZZAR'S DREAM

In your vision, O King, you saw a statue, very large
and exceedingly bright, terrifying in appearance.

Severed
head and legs
in the shadow of the rock
that severed them.

Till noon
it is cool,
after which
the land turns
into a furnace.

*

At evening: distorted
shadows of the vanquished giant.

In the chest I feel heat
throbbing.

In the head the still
desert humming
with one thought:

the dark hot
idea of sun.

Skull: its golden gutted cavity—
essential barrenness
of mouth and eye holes—

fills
with blown
sand.

*

The late
rain gives
iron limbs
a dried blood
patina.

In the narrow
cavernous leg
I am the marrow.

The idea's
analgesic—

to pace
the roomless
raw tube.

*

An experiment:

Stay in the head all day.
Know the amplified heat.
Perhaps begin to believe
that all is fire, one form
and everywhere.

What conforms to what?

Idea / object—

Arrows
of adequation
at both ends.

*

One evening after another.

A brand
upon the imagined;
an obsidian star
from the fixed heavens
smoking in the earth.

*

I rise
from silver ribs
to witness the moon
white in a white dry sea.

The censure of sand.

*

I've slept more than three days
in every part of this whale-like body
beached and broken in the desert.

A pacing idea.

*

Last night a million bells of different timbres—

rain abrading the gold forehead,
thinner in places than I thought,
the smith having pounded
the expense out
to its finest extent.

Rain ran into eye holes—
backward,
as if the changing world wept
into its changeless idea.

*

The punch in the shoulder,
where the tip of the mountain
brought the god down,
has become my chair.

At evening I climb abrasions and dents
to sit in silver
and watch the desert night.

At the synapse between vision and sleep:

A glissando of stars
congealing into one
immense glittering cross.

*

Wind sings into the mouth,
howls, cries into the mouth
gravid
with the memory of some
first sea.

*

Lightning plays in figural flashings
against arcing walls of silver and gold—
rude cuneiform,
mercurial
at the synapses of beauty.

*

Sunrise,
and truth
is declarative being.

Exceedingly bright,
terrifying
in appearance.

The terrifying sound
of the past
or the future
falling.

The rain
of matter upon sense
destroys me momently.

*

I dream the statue intact
deep in the womb of the mountain.

The mountain
holds him
as he holds
the mountain.

*

Something small
to hold to.
This morning

sparkling hems
on slips of water
ran one

over the other
down the smooth
black rock.

*

I circle the shards,
the body of that head.

My footprints about
those pieces of feet.

*Hands unreasonable
never to touch.*

*

The stillness at the center of any
abandoned wreckage.

Stillness and heat become a vast presence.

*Perhaps God does not so much break into reality
as intensify it.*

*

What
have I loved
by these measures?

Philosophy: flour
blown into the face
of the starving man
who asked for bread.

*

The eyes tear up trying for the horizon.

A tiny red flower
out of evening's
lustrous flux.

*

Wait in the body.

Human ruin
gathered at the nadir of the desert's
long blue pause.

Perhaps God breaks into reality.

*

Black ants
climb the cactus,
ascend and descend
their acrid
ladder to heaven.

*

Clouds are gathering in blue
oblongs, ranked
across the east

from this rock,
from this mountain.

To come to the point
where there is no choice
and then to make a choice.

Hold out your hands and be led
where you do not want to go.

Go over without calculation.

*

Everyone
a part of the purge.

*So they showed themselves free
of my willfulness.*

*

Life spent separating
the clean from the unclean
with my own hands.

From calculation
into the ocean
where even I

am separable.

*

Flesh
against the waves;

thrown to be broken.

*

Flesh is place and
the consequent ache;

flesh drapes time
and washes away.

In space a
betrayal
of distance imposed.

*

I in she—

it serves me.

I won't see a dove
from my dark pulpit.

*

Little myths
(I miss home).

Earth embraced water
so deeply it rose up
out of its own dry door
and took rain into its leafy arms.

*

Don't talk to me about substantial forms.

Diving, I go
to the roots of the mountains,

the veiled substratum.

*

Rising I see or imagine I see
silvery water spread horizonless before the wind.

Light discloses light, layered toward evening.

Light distends in distraction toward heat.

*

The horizon held
in thrall.

Erect from the grave-wash
a mental mast.

Eidetic
steps
the eye
ascends.

*

A plume
of water

thunders
above me.

*

This rivering between naught and naught.

I cannot keep two moments together.

*

Womb-wash.

Perpetual
nascence.

*

A million
minnows
pour in
over my head.

Wet twisting stars,

or the children
of stars.

Waters
above the floodgates
of the firmament.

*

To think is to thirst.

*

To come to the point
where what is utterly
determined
gives you freedom.

*

Lapping shadows ashen in the starlight.

Scales fall in the ribbed leaves falling.

ELIJAH'S CAVE

At least know this: when I saw the sun
I did not start back,

but afterwards, after the slaughter,
I fell prey to a second kind of blindness.

*

The cave comes after the sun,
after the torque of muscle
at man's apex. After the flourish,
after the bold prayer,
the unworldly assurance of prayer.

How I called out like Adam imagining
the inner twist of things—

melody and tendon
transparent under the bright-
tipped syllables.

*

I have given up on well-kempt thought. My mind
a matted tangle,

a new place in fear.

*

Below, the blue
cut of the canyon

and above,
the great luminous mind
of the thunderhead.

Long sweeping blue-gray rain
sliced by lightning.

Cliff wall becomes
waterfall
and cave

a cup
of air.

*

What does night keep
that day in its vaunting
relinquishes?

*

Shall I say that love and blood
are the same? The sacrament
passes over,
aches ahead of itself
toward...

I am tired of the future. Tired
of the arrow that goes on and on.

*

At the mouth
different grasses
alive in the night,
in the spicy air.

The still small voice is not
a vagary of God. Its smallness
is its specificity

through that exact tangle
of sagebrush. In that crushed
scent of pale gray sage.

THE ANGEL

Do you know the difference
between a word

and the descriptive
shadows of a word?

Perfect as act
not adjective.

Mind alone as wing.

*

An untoward attainment in a culture
of creative lostness.

Are demons the deeper
need of your shadow side?

Close-held loneliness folded over fear.

*

The moral mathematician
calls the Fall into his figures
as if genius required it,

but I have seen creative genius

ringed in single meaning,
lambent in its reach.

*

Neither supplement
nor substitute

in the darkening air.

Exousia—

a breathing bridge
where bowed wings dive.

*

Head lights and tail lights—
lava lines that rise
and fall on the hill
of holy fire. Series S—
the whole
sibilance seen
at once, the whole

curving
causal chain
helplessly contingent.

*

The Fall—
buried in splinters and springs.

*

Breaking a word makes light
shining back upon wholeness.

A

up-
turns
into

V

Do you know the difference
between completion and the broken
idea of completion?

*

Even in reason
a basic brokenness
crippled of breath,

distillate
dismemberment,

a walking without . . .

The absence cannot
in light of absence
be defined.

Inverse fullness
in the chasm of should-have,

the ghostly glut
of what is not.

Arid-blue betweenness.

*

The fine
capillaried limbs
of the Russian olives, fan

to a low gray haze
floating through the pines,
wreathing the more solid green.

Matter sifts
down below substance,
lingers at the shift.

*

The petals
of every image
fall off.

Who
flayed away to air
would speak in the voice of an angel?

*

It's all straw.

Yet blown about
from the center,
something
catches;

some straw
spun gold
touches the others.

*

You are deep in the burn of history.

A raw kinetics
way way off in what is here.

PART II

GATHERINGS AT THE CUSP

I

Has it all been an atmosphere
you walked through, aesthetic
accident made even of
the prophet's blood-soaked railing,
rhapsodic red through which
the words have gone on walking,
stained for the evening as tongues
are stained by wine,
for the ease of the evening,
for a presumed loosening against the true
undoing? What gets through
the sunset to color the morning window?
Blood of Christ blood of Christ my eyes

2

The birth pangs shall come for him
The chains lay under the bale
and are hooked up back side
but when it is time he shall not
so that when the pneumatic
hoists the chains the bale
is lifted and tipped
out
present himself
The layered
craving crushed, blocked
bound with wires
where children break forth

(After Hosea 13:15)

3

Display display
display dis-
play. The retail pace
erased me. *You
wanted the giddy
freneticism—a free
range drug.*
All day tunes
with no room in them.
*Fodder for your brittle
humor.* My anger.

4

What did I
hold out for?
What did you hold?
Twenty five years an object
was object alone.
A piece of gravel
as easily thrown
as not.
The gavel comes down hard.
Come on, you too,
you, you want the wanting
alone.

5

Mind made
in the image
of my hands.
To understand
means to read
what is inside a thing.
Born to think
we all seek ways
not to think at all.
Read: a series
of facile distractions,
a flattened pantomime.
Form, form, the inner-
outline. Intus
legere . . . No,
my night-numb,
knotted, fumble-dumb
hands.

(After Thomas Aquinas, Disputed Questions on Truth, *Question 1, art. 12)*

6

A blade
of light slides
across the slate-
colored wall.
*When does guilt
assign fate?*
Prayed
*Blood of Christ
Blood of Christ.*
My eyes
level
with the floor
caught
at the side
the hem
of a blue robe.

7

Abraham's hand
stayed.
God himself shall offer
God himself. The power
that plies the sacrifice;
the approach
as sign.
Melechizedeck—*Melek*
shalom—lifted bread and wine,
touched
in sight
the mountains.
Ache of space created
in forethought of its broaching.

8

Wheat of the
Saint, beaten,
ground in the lion's
mouth, to be
flour for hosts.
Be then the wine
in your despite.
No trust beyond
my night-live
lust, my hungering
haste.
A distillation,
then, a spirit
squeezed
from the base.

(After Ignatius of Antioch)

9

A music
than which none greater
can be conceived, and which cannot
be conceived not
to exist, played
in the mind of a humble
custodian who mumbles
more than hums.
A deceiver: the voice
incoherent when received
by the air. The music
is not really there. Ah,
and I thought you a believer.

(After Anslem's proof)

Wall of wavering
aridity
where the voice
has dried, stuck
to the flat horizon. Struck,
and all that water
and all that broke.
Blue-white hem
fronting the desert.

Have I sent the sun out of me,
bright arc that centered me,
sun my mother tended?
Circulatio entium . . . actually,
a street person on his seventh
circle. *Even when you slept*
in the valley of the shadow
you felt the warmth
like sacramental blood
rayed out at consecration.

12

Time's best measure is the rate
at which our wounds heal.
How long the wounds of state
stay open, fester
even in the grave.
You think then we are done?
I think the test
of our first measure
is still beyond completion;
I think we are still bleeding.
Always will be. Only one thing
to be done with blood
else we will never heal, and our time
perpetually repealed.

13

Running through the graveyard
I saw the fanning form
of the phoenix in broken
pine sprays. And in an oil stain
a raven. *Ah,*
a strange place of signification.
Dreamless daylight,
Steubenville, Ohio.
It was no accident
that on that run
you hurt your hip,
and will not run again.
The wind will blow
from other lips.
You will not escape from this
so easily.

14

Brandon died from Ocean
as if he could see the waves
from here. In the highway's
concrete caves,
dozens of old cans
of Aqua Net,
the dispensers bit off.
The muffled ache came clear
under the wailing headlights.
*Springtime offers pasques
and autumn purple asters
wild and sudden and still
on the highway's
dirty embankments.*

15

I saw Eric
by Stoute's Creek
living where
the road goes
under the water
and rises
to the next hill.
He smiled at me,
the long
cancer gone
from his body.
I forgive
you the turning
when we
were twelve
and friend-
ship starved.

16

What kind of famine we are in,
nor for bread nor for water,
but for hearing healing.
The starved air carries
a resonance, a ray
of the summer-sung blood
the prophet thought would pour
from the hills. Florid orchestra
floods the evening with bewildering
moods. These layered fomentations
will not satiate. *I hear*
one bottom note, no more,
night-long
and undiminished.

(After Amos 9 : 11–12)

17

Even refuse of the wheat we sell. Husks
trussed up as real food. Gatherings at the cusp
of our country's wavering age. Many lusts
whirling in the heat and wanting
to pierce the light-
bulb. They flit and yet
like secret burrs, pit
the mind. I do nothing but sit
and read. Hunger, hunger
ingrown upon emptiness.
A windless twist
of glitter
moves across the desert.

(After Amos 8 : 6)

18

"Love the tee shirt." Above
the mushroom cloud: *Made
in America,* and below it:
Tested in Japan. The bomb—
inevitable as the opening
of Pandora's box. It is an issue
other than this
lacking of gravity, as if
one had never looked
into another pair of eyes
and seen the soul as any
soul. *Do not cry,
not yet, for you shall have to cry
from another wound.*

(After Dante, Purgatorio, *Canto 30 : 55–57)*

19

From Juan
Diego's open
tilma, the slips
still spill. From petals
her face. Petals
from the purity
of her face.
It is a circle
then, concealing
revealing
concealing . . .
ingrown upon emptiness.
It is the sun
my mother tended.
A crucifix a-
cross her.
A great
gold light
behind her.

20

The ploughman shall overtake
the reaper
and children break forth.
A myth as old
as Ovid. Ah, then you imply
it's older still, and deeper.
No one ploughs that way
nor sings as he sows.
"The Plough and the Song"
is a painting by Arshile Gorky.
His mother witnessed
the Armenian genocide.
His pouring colors washed
the prophet's hills.
His painting was another way
to cry.

(After Amos 9 : 13)

21

Low saffron clouds
sail, sheer, pierced
by rose rays.
To the sides, distinct strings
of blue rain. *Ah,*
a Maxfield Parrish
moment, a pretty girl
waiting in the wings.
Notice the show
and tell of the Spirit—
the only one who can work
from whole cloth.
It's just another painting.
Another painting: "The Way
My Mother's Apron Strings
Unfold in My Life."

22

Old burns, faded stains
through crude
cloth woven
of cactus fiber.
The tilma *was*
his work apron.
Holy by what seems life
after life
of looking.
And the other
sweat-soaked side?
His all is inside
out, in the angel's
paint. *Prime,*
Lord, the raw
side of me.

23

Sun
my mother tended
whose rays are roots
that stem and flower in midair.
Sky itself the *tilma* tumbling petals,
petals pressed by memory
into blue folds.
San Diego, make it new.

24

Springtime and the natural world passes
through the sweet clean wounds
of Francis. Flames
of Indian paintbrush
red to the canyon's edge. *I felt him*
to the reaches of my body.
Under the elevated Sangres,
to the reaches of the sky.

25

The edge
of the future is nothing but the edge
of the worn-out past.
But you forget:
the future could come
from a source entirely other,
racing toward us.
It is, then, an exterior,
disasters often are.
Exterior implies interior;
grace exchanges place with fate.
Random in the random terror.
The bright reach
of hands in babble's despite.

26

Tiers
of sound. Hear-
ing healing. Humming
bird wings above
the bottom note: *I will send you
Elijah*
across pentecostal
waters. Anti-babble,
this lifting,
shimmering
gathering
pool of tongues.

(After Malachi 3 : 23)

PART III

POEMS FOR THE FEAST OF CORPUS CHRISTI

The lamb the lamp alone

I

Gabriel's words:
a gold
ribbon of syllables
on a gold ground that contains
Angel and Mary.

"What is a sacrament but a kind of visible word."

Radiant
ratio.

2

Eva

     Ave
     Ave

        Maria

The turning of
momentous yes
as on a fulcrum
toward the right.

"Unalloyed joy"
at a point
polar to its
darkened sister.

3

On the small
altar

the burning rose
candle reflects

off the icon's
lacquer

flame
and flame's

namesake: Spirit
come

upon Mary come
upon these

gifts, to make
them holy.

4

Sapientia
Sophia Seat

         of wisdom. Mother
         of the Word.

Sapientia
Sapere Taste

         to

         see.

5

They laid him
in a manger,

a feeding
trough.

Take
and eat. The splayed

limbs came
down

by ropes
slowly

into the arms
of another Joseph.

6

This is   This is

                The heaviness
                entoils us

                unless
                it is lifted.

                This
                our body.

7

The priest   makes sacred

caesuras,

leans
over and speaks

closely and slowly
into the host.

O laving
Logos over-
pouring.

Create in me   Create in me

Listen

God's
voice over
the face

of this
deep.

8

To the north

        Kenosis the key note

To the south

        The vestments of the voice
        sound over all
        singularities

To the east

        Logos
        enhosted

To the west

        The heart made naked
        when the name takes clothes

9

Sarcasm
thwarts
ascendancy

as it does

    the body.

        How light,
        Merton wrote,
        the host
            lifted
        in consecration.

10

White with
figural flashings.

Hidden,
the hidden image. Peter's recognition

and ours

                    under the elements.

The turning
monstrance, a light-
house with its tended
fire.

                    Rayed
            in ecclesial
                        release.

Still and radiant voice
turning through the room.

II

Kate said when she was away
from her children
a week or more
it was no longer enough
to simply see
them, she wanted
to taste them.

Lumen

Christi,

lambent

Spirit from her eyes,
from the whole host
of her face.

12

Via and *vita* the same word.

Don't complete the project for yourself.

Viaticum:
bread for the way.

Not wisdom literature.

13

With what tenderness the workmen wrapped
the wooden Corpus in white cloth
to keep the sawdust off
while cutting the cross.

> *Trasumanar*

>> Because the form
>> is not proportionate to the matter
>> but pours as love pours over.

Now the new tabernacle
at its elevated base.

>> The host-cross raised.

14

<pre>
                    I
      Lucenti   M
                    M
                    A   Incendi
                    N
      Dello   U
                    E   Spirito
                    L

              Santo
</pre>

15

Mind as scribe. Many minds

logoi

        from whom an intelligible love

                spirates.

        Oceanic fervor
        in the small circled form.

NOTES

The author is indebted to the following sources: Walter Wangerin, Jr., for "The Night Watch"; Jay S. Samuels for "In Nebuchadnezzar's Dream"; Yvor Winters for "In Nebuchadnezzar's Dream."

ABOUT THE AUTHOR

David Mutschlecner lives and works in New Mexico. His books, which include *Veils* (Stride Press) and *Esse* (Ahsahta Press), seek to harmonize the personal and the theological. His master's degree from Saint John's College in Santa Fe reflects an enduring love for the poetry alive in philosophy as its ever-fresh first question.

Ahsahta Press

SAWTOOTH POETRY PRIZE SERIES

2002: Aaron McCollough, *Welkin* (Brenda Hillman, judge)

2003: Graham Foust, *Leave the Room to Itself* (Joe Wenderoth, judge)

2004: Noah Eli Gordon, *The Area of Sound Called the Subtone* (Claudia Rankine, judge)

2005: Karla Kelsey, *Knowledge, Forms, The Aviary* (Carolyn Forché, judge)

2006: Paige Ackerson-Kiely, *In No One's Land* (D.A. Powell, judge)

NEW SERIES

1. Lance Phillips, *Corpus Socius*
2. Heather Sellers, *Drinking Girls and Their Dresses*
3. Lisa Fishman, *Dear, Read*
4. Peggy Hamilton, *Forbidden City*
5. Dan Beachy-Quick, *Spell*
6. Liz Waldner, *Saving the Appearances*
7. Charles O. Hartman, *Island*
8. Lance Phillips, *Cur aliquid vidi*
9. Sandra Miller, *Oriflamme*
10. Brigitte Byrd, *Fence Above the Sea*
11. Ethan Paquin, *The Violence*
12. Ed Allen, *67 Mixed Messages*
13. Brian Henry, *Quarantine*
14. Kate Greenstreet, *case sensitive*
15. Aaron McCollough, *Little Ease*
16. Susan Tichy, *Bone Pagoda*
17. Susan Briante, *Pioneers in the Study of Motion*
18. Lisa Fishman, *The Happiness Experiment*
19. Heidi Lynn Staples, *Dog Girl*
20. David Mutschlecner, *Esse*

Ahsahta Press

MODERN AND CONTEMPORARY POETRY OF THE AMERICAN WEST

Sandra Alcosser, *A Fish to Feed All Hunger*

David Axelrod, *Jerusalem of Grass*

David Baker, *Laws of the Land*

Dick Barnes, *Few and Far Between*

Conger Beasley, Jr., *Over DeSoto's Bones*

Linda Bierds, *Flights of the Harvest-Mare*

Richard Blessing, *Winter Constellations*

Boyer, Burmaster, and Trusky, eds., *The Ahsahta Anthology*

Peggy Pond Church, *New and Selected Poems*

Katharine Coles, *The One Right Touch*

Wyn Cooper, *The Country of Here Below*

Craig Cotter, *Chopstix Numbers*

Judson Crews, *The Clock of Moss*

H.L. Davis, *Selected Poems*

Susan Strayer Deal, *The Dark is a Door*

Susan Strayer Deal, *No Moving Parts*

Linda Dyer, *Fictional Teeth*

Gretel Ehrlich, *To Touch the Water*

Gary Esarey, *How Crows Talk and Willows Walk*

Julie Fay, *Portraits of Women*

Thomas Hornsby Ferril, *Anvil of Roses*

Thomas Hornsby Ferril, *Westering*

Hildegarde Flanner, *The Hearkening Eye*

Charley John Greasybear, *Songs*

Corrinne Hales, *Underground*

Hazel Hall, *Selected Poems*

Nan Hannon, *Sky River*

Gwendolen Haste, *Selected Poems*

Kevin Hearle, *Each Thing We Know Is Changed Because We Know It And Other Poems*

Sonya Hess, *Kingdom of Lost Waters*

Cynthia Hogue, *The Woman in Red*

Robert Krieger, *Headlands, Rising*

Elio Emiliano Ligi, *Disturbances*

Haniel Long, *My Seasons*

Ken McCullough, *Sycamore•Oriole*

Norman McLeod, *Selected Poems*

Barbara Meyn, *The Abalone Heart*

David Mutschlecner, *Esse*

Dixie Partridge, *Deer in the Haystacks*

Gerrye Payne, *The Year-God*

George Perreault, *Curved Like an Eye*

Howard W. Robertson, *to the fierce guard in the Assyrian Saloon*

Leo Romero, *Agua Negra*

Leo Romero, *Going Home Away Indian*

Miriam Sagan, *The Widow's Coat*

Philip St. Clair, *At the Tent of Heaven*

Philip St. Clair, *Little-Dog-of-Iron*

Donald Schenker, *Up Here*

Gary Short, *Theory of Twilight*

D.J. Smith, *Prayers for the Dead Ventriloquist*

Richard Speakes, *Hannah's Travel*

Genevieve Taggard, *To the Natural World*

Tom Trusky, ed., *Women Poets of the West*

Marnie Walsh, *A Taste of the Knife*

Bill Witherup, *Men at Work*

Carolyne Wright, *Stealing the Children*

This book is set in Apollo MT type with Emigre MrsEaves titles
by Ahsahta Press at Boise State University
and manufactured according to the Green Press Initiative
by Thomson-Shore, Inc.
Cover design by Quemadura.
Book design by Janet Holmes.

AHSAHTA PRESS

2007

JANET HOLMES, DIRECTOR

STEFFEN BROWN

NAOMI TARLE

JR WALSH

DENNIS BARTON, INTERN

DALE SPANGLER, INTERN